Be Extraordinary

Be Extraordinary
Your Guide To Self-Mastery

BRANDON EASTMAN

Contents

Introduction: What is an 'Extraordinary Life?' 1

Chapter 1: Emotional Mastery 5

Chapter 2: Physical Mastery 23

Chapter 3: Financial Mastery 49

Chapter 4: Relationship Mastery 67

Chapter 5: Spiritual Mastery 83

Conclusion 91

About the Author 96

INTRODUCTION
What is an 'Extraordinary Life?'

THE DEFINITION OF extraordinary is **'*very unusual, or remarkable.*'** Few pursue an extraordinary life, and even fewer understand what it consists of. We all want to live an extraordinary life and be 'happy', but everyone defines that word differently too. What does it take for YOU to be happy? What does an extraordinary life look like to YOU?

The title of this book is intentional: This is for those who aren't looking for the 'normal', society-pressured path through life. They're not looking for average. They understand there is unlimited potential inside of them NOW! If you're holding this book, there's a great chance this perfectly describes you! Congratulations, you've made a big step. There are thousands of books out there teaching the principles on how to become successful and live a fulfilling life. In this book, I will go over the tips and strategies that I've found to work, which have propelled me to success in my own life. I am grateful to have the opportunity to share them with you.

An extraordinary life is doing what I want, when I want, with whomever I want, however I want to do it, all while providing value and giving to others! A remarkable life is having the freedom to travel with my family around the world, while creating an impact on the lives of millions, and helping others to make the changes and improvements that I've been able to make in my own life. To live an extraordinary life, we must focus on self-mastery. Self-mastery is mastering each key area of life: our emotions, finances, relationships, spirituality, and physical health.

Achieving self-mastery equates to obtaining extraordinary results. Living an extraordinary life comes down to mastering the key areas we are about to discuss. Each area is as important as the next because if one gets out of balance, it throws the others out of balance. So, is it possible to have perfect balance in each area? I would say no. To lead an extraordinary life, we must learn to 'counterbalance' what is important to us. It comes down to prioritizing what is most important in your life at any given time. As you dive in and discover the strategies in these 5 areas of life, ask yourself, "What is most important to **ME?**"

You may read this book in whichever way you like: some will read it chapter by chapter, word for word. For many, the most effective use of your time would be to define which of the 6 Key Areas you most need to focus on and improve. You may be asking, "How would I know that?" Let's find out together! We will be discussing emotional, physical, financial, relational, and spiritual mastery. I recommend asking yourself the question, ***"Of these 5 areas, which is the one that I can focus on, such that by doing so, everything else will be easier or unnec-essary?"*** Gary Keller, author of the book *The One Thing,* calls this the Focusing Question. The quality of the questions you ask will result in the quality of the answer you receive. If you want better answers, ask a better question! This is a question that covers all your bases when asked repeatedly.

After each section, you will be given a 7-Day Challenge. Reading this book in its entirety may help you and give you some ideas on how to live a better life. Those who follow this book chapter by chapter and complete the Challenges as they go will notice a difference in daily performance. For maximum results, ***play full out!*** That means taking the time to complete the 7-Day Challenge after you complete each section, then re-visit this book once you have completed each Challenge. If you forget to follow through or fail in its undertaking, you must re-start the 7 days! Do you accept?

Reading books is a beautiful habit to acquire. It is a way for the author to condense decades of their life's experience, so the reader may spend a few days digesting it through their words and stories. Understand, however, that knowledge alone is **NOT** power. Knowledge is only *potential* power: it will only create results in your life when you USE it! ***Execution*** is the ultimate power! ***Complexity*** is the enemy of execution. If something is too complex, or too much at once, our brains will shut down at the sight of it and we will never take action. Start with the one Key Area that focusing on will make the others easier or unnecessary, and also take action during the 7-Day Challenge following each chapter. ***This*** is how you will achieve extraordinary results in your life!

CHAPTER 1
Emotional Mastery

"Your emotions are the slaves to your thoughts, and you are the slave to your emotions."

– Elizabeth Gilbert,
Eat Pray Love

I BELIEVE THAT EVERYTHING begins with our thoughts and our way of thinking. Let's talk about what a thought actually is. A thought is the formation of opinions, especially as a philosophy or system of ideas, or the opinions so formed. How does a thought occur? We see something, such as a person or thing, or maybe someone is speaking to us. We might smell something that we remember from our past, which causes us to feel a certain way. Has this ever happened to you? Any external stimulus causes us to think a thought. After we think a thought, we attach a meaning to it. As someone says something to you, you immediately, and usually subconsciously, create a meaning in your mind. This happens so fast we rarely notice it. If someone insults you, you may attach a negative meaning. That meaning might be, "That person doesn't know who I am. They don't understand me, who do they think they are saying something like that to me?" Or, if someone compliments you, that meaning might be, "This is a nice person. This is a genuine person. This is someone who cares about me." The meaning we attach to something then triggers an emotion: and your emotions hold extreme power. Your emotions determine the action you will take! And your choices and actions determine the way your life unfolds before you.

That was a lot, so let's revisit it: An event or external stimuli occurs, and you think a thought. You attach a meaning to this thought. And from that meaning comes an emotion. Whether that emotion is positive or negative, you will take a unique action. If it's a positive, empowering emotion, your actions are most likely going to be positive and constructive. These actions will serve you, and others. They will bring abundance into your life. They will bring you more feelings of happiness and fulfillment. If it's a negative emotion, you will act negatively. You're going to think bad thoughts. You're going to be the person that other people won't want to spend time around. And because you're thinking negative thoughts, you will continue attracting more negative thoughts into your life. Think of your thoughts like a magnet: what you send out, you'll attract back to you.

Is it true that a positive situation to one person could mean a negative situation to someone else? Of course! It's all about the meaning that we attach to the situation. We have the personal power to give whatever meaning we want to any situation. You can't control the outside circumstances or stimuli in your life. You can't control the weather, or taxes, or the attitude of your neighbor. But the one thing you can always control is the meaning you attach to these circumstances. Because you can control the meaning, you can control the emotion that manifests. Because you now control the emotion, you will have personal power over the actions you take, and how you react to any situation. This is exciting because this means you have complete and total power over your life!

> *"I don't want to be at the mercy of my emotions. I want to use them, to enjoy them, and to dominate them."*
>
> *– Oscar Wilde*

Let's paint a picture of this: I want you to imagine your mind as a mental factory. Inside this factory, your thoughts are the workers. The factory is run by two foremen; their names are Mr. Triumph and Mr. Defeat. The workers and the thoughts you have 'feed' the foremen. When you think more positive thoughts, Mr. Triumph is fed. Mr. Triumph begins to dominate the factory. When he dominates the factory you have better experiences. You feel better. And because you feel better, you take different actions, and more positive things happen in your life. People who feed Mr. Triumph say things like, "I can do this. This is something that I can figure out. I don't know how we're going to get this done, but I know that where there's a will there's a way. I have no doubt in my mind that we will succeed." However, those who feed Mr. Defeat cause Mr. Defeat to grow and dominate the factory. When that happens you think more negative thoughts. You think, "Oh, I can never achieve this. How are we going to do this? This task is impossible." Because they have those negative thoughts, Mr. Defeat runs the show.

It is completely in your power to determine the thoughts that you think daily. When someone says, "That's impossible," they are putting their beliefs on display. This is a disempowering belief. Because this person has the belief that whatever they're trying to accomplish is impossible, the action that they put towards that situation is going to be lesser because they don't believe that it can be done. Let's take a look at an example of this:

Roger Banister was the first person ever to run the four-minute mile. For hundreds of years people have tried to run the four-minute mile, yet never succeeded. After a while, they deemed it an impossibility. Roger Banister didn't see this as impossible. Every single day he fed Mr. Triumph and he thought things like, "I can do this. This must be possible." He asked himself questions like, "How is it that I can accomplish this? I don't know how I'm going to achieve it, but there must be a way." Because he thought these things every single day, Roger visualized himself successfully running the four-minute mile to achieve a sense of belief and certainty in his mind and body. He visualized himself crossing that finish line before the four-minute mark. Then he ran, every single day. He had the positive thought which led to action every day. He practiced, and practiced, and practiced, and guess what eventually happened? Roger Banister successfully ran the four-minute mile and was the first person ever to accomplish it.

What was once deemed impossible was proven to be possible. Someone did it, and because someone did it, within a year after Roger Banister ran the four-minute mile, twenty-four other people ran the four-minute mile. In that same year. What does this tell you? What it tells me is something is only impossible until someone proves it otherwise. Something is only impossible until someone does it. Remember, your thoughts feed the foreman. The minute you say, "I can't do this," you won't be able to. Like Henry Ford once said, "Whether you say that you can, or you can't, you are always right." The language we tell ourselves will determine the outcome.

Whenever you're confronted with a challenge or obstacle in whatever you're trying to accomplish, whether it's getting yourself out of debt and amassing a fortune; losing the weight and getting the body you want to have; or acquiring the relationships you want to have, the first thing we must do is develop the belief that it can be done. Because where positive beliefs lie, positive thoughts lie. Where you have positive thoughts, you have actions that reflect those thoughts. These actions lead to extraordinary results.

The next question is, what impacts your thought? What causes you to think positively and what causes you to think negatively? There are many things, but we'll talk about just a few here. One thing that heavily affects your thoughts, whether you're thinking positively or negatively, are your peer groups and friends. The people you spend time around. We're going to talk about this in a later chapter.

Your environment determines the way you think. If you're continuously watching the news daily, how will you feel? What are the main subjects that the news talks about? It talks about death, fires, robbery, poverty and all the negative things happening in the world. Because of this, you don't hear about all the amazing things happening. You don't hear about all the massive donations contributed by billionaires to third-world countries. You don't hear about the schools being built there, either. You don't hear about the daily acts of kindness because those things don't sell. The news doesn't buy positive stories because they don't deliver the same 'shock value' as the negative content.

The small percentage of us who monitor our thoughts and foster empowering beliefs have the obligation to serve the rest of the world. That's why you're reading this right now! You are reading this book because you are in the small percentage of people who are going to make a difference. You are an entrepreneur. You are an inventor. You are a maker of change or a titan of industry. You are someone who is going to make a difference.

Because of all this, it's very important that we monitor what we let into our world. "Be the guardian to the door of your mind" is a beautiful quote from personal development guru Jim Rohn, who understood these concepts, and shared them with the world while he was with us. Continuously monitor the environment you are in and the people you spend time around. They influence your emotional state. Your emotional state determines your mental health.

What else can affect your thought? The foods you eat. If you eat junk food regularly or you overeat, you might feel good temporarily because you traded short-term pleasure for long-term pain. The foods you eat determine the way you feel. Your brain takes up 1/50th of your entire body. However, your brain consumes 1/5th of all the calories you consume. What does this tell you? This means that the quality of the food you eat determines the quality of your thoughts, and as a result, the quality of your actions. How you take care of your body determines your emotional state.

The way you move your body also deter-mines your state. Emotion stands for 'Energy in Motion.' If you sit on the couch all day you will be in a very different state than if you stood up, jumped around, and went for a jog outside. Maybe you go to play basketball, or a sport with friends and get around positive influences and like-minds. Maybe you go to the gym and you exercise there or run on the treadmill. Do whatever it takes to stay active because your physical state determines your thoughts.

> *We are all beings of immense power and potential; the Greats learn how to harness and USE this power!*
>
> *– Brandon Eastman*

Another way to improve your emotional mastery is to develop a morning and nighttime routine. Your morning and your night are the two areas of your life you can control. Think about this: what do most people do when they wake up in the morning? Let's say they work at 9:00 AM. Most people, if their drive to work is 30 minutes, will wake up at 8:00 AM, and immediately grab their phone and get their dopamine rush by checking Facebook, their emails, and other social media.

They'll then jump in the shower, and afterwards might scarf down a quick breakfast, usually of energy-poor foods. Then they hop in their car and they head to the office. They work until 5:00 PM, they come home, they watch TV, they grab a drink (maybe even an alcoholic one), they eat their dinner, and they go to bed. The next day, they repeat. The cycle goes on and on.

Let's look at this person. How do we think they feel throughout their day? How do we think they feel about their life? This could be a great individual, and a great friend; I am not discounting that. But that doesn't mean they live the best life they could be. What are the long-term consequences of this lifestyle? Because of their low-quality routine, we can confidently say this person's lifespan will not be as long as someone who takes care of their body, their mind, and finds fulfillment through a morning and nighttime routine. Do you believe that you're worth this time of self-love?

Let's take a look at someone else: this person works at 9:00 AM, and instead of getting up at 8:00 AM, they woke up an hour earlier, at 7 AM. Nothing crazy, right? Nothing too difficult. They wake up, get out of bed, wash off their face, maybe hop around a little or dance to get the blood flowing. They may even throw on some shoes to go outside for a brisk walk or a 20-minute jog.

They get themselves sweating almost immediately after they rose for the day. When they sweat, they release endorphins and growth hormones, which make them feel confident and amazing. Releasing all of these amazing feelings in their body will prime them for your entire day. After their walk or a jog, they come back home, eat some fruit, hydrate their body, and head to work. How do you think the quality of their performance will now be at work, considering how they prepared themselves? Astounding, right?

They get home from work. They might go to the gym for a second wind exercise, maybe lifting weights this time around. They have dinner with their family, a nice healthy, combined meal, and before they go to bed, they read a good book or listen to some audiotapes to feed their mind. Right before they go to bed, they think about one thing that happened during the day they can be absolutely and utterly grateful for.

Let's take a look at these two individuals: How do we think the two of those people feel as a result of their routines? How are they **different?**

I can almost guarantee that they're different in every area of their life, and self-mastery. They're different in their relationships, they're different in their physical body and their health. They're different in their financial situations. It's a given. The individual in the second example has a tighter grasp on the outcome of their life. You can't control what happens to you during your day. You can't control the phone calls, you can't control the emails, you can't control the person cutting you off in traffic. The one thing you *can* control is your morning and nighttime routine.

What kind of difference can this make over the course of a year, or even 10 years? Let's look at our two examples: The first individual? Morbidly obese. Their family's just like them, because they're the leader and they impact their family's decisions. They watch the negative news, they don't read any kind of self-development books, or any books in their field to develop their skills. They have a victim mindset. They believe that everything happens to them, versus for them.

How about the second individual? They're in shape, they have no debts, they're continuously building their freedom fund (which we'll cover a bit later), they have strong emotional relationships with the people they care about, they positively influence those at home, and the groups they inhabit. This person experiences life in a different way than the first example. Develop a strong morning and nighttime routine, and it will change your entire life.

Feeding your mind with influences that can help it grow is another way to master your emotional state. Imagine watching the news and taking in that negative information. Then imagine reading a book on how to control your emotional state, like you're doing right now. You are feeding your mind with information that will help you regulate your thoughts throughout the entire day to serve you.

What happens when you read a book is interesting; your mind looks at the words and digests the information that you're reading. Your brain doesn't know the difference between whether you created that information or if it was created by someone else. Your brain doesn't know that someone else wrote this book. Your brain is digesting this information as if you created it, and because of that, you're encoding that information into your mind over the course of time.

Think of the impact that reading 30 minutes every single night can make in your life! Imagine digesting that positive information every night over the course of 5 or 10 years! You'll completely change the trajectory of your life for the better.

This is emotional mastery. The moment you take control of the meanings you assign to external stimuli, that's when you have the personal power to take control of your life. That is the moment you'll head toward your dreams and achieve whatever you set out to do.

Your 7-Day Challenge to Emotional Mastery!

I want you to write down every emotion you have felt in the past WEEK. You may have felt happy, sad, frustrated, ecstatic, bored, exuberant, magnificent, etc. Write down each and every feeling you have experienced! Take a few minutes and do this NOW.

Generally, if you come up with a list of 7-10 emotions, your experience of life is blander than someone who has come up with 20-30 emotions or MORE! Is that always true? Of course not. But that is what you'll usually find. More emotions simply mean more options for how to feel! Because remember, you can feel however you want, whenever you want! Fewer emotions, means fewer options for how to feel, and unless they're ALL great emotions, I don't want to be stranded with only a handful of ways to feel! Right? Work to expand your emotional options and recognize how each emotional state feels different to you.

This is your Challenge! Throughout the next 7 days, remember to ask yourself, "How am I feeling right now?" If the answer is bad, it means your thoughts are bad. If you feel great, it means the same goes for your thoughts. If you are feeling bad, or aren't feeling any certain way in particular, it means you're thinking of things that aren't serving you! Here, ask yourself the above question so you can recognize the state you're in NOW, then think of something that has made you feel VERY happy, and notice the difference in the way you feel, and even how you're using your body!

Sometimes, it's very difficult to change a negative thought, to a positive one. I have found a process that works very well for me, called 'Reframing.' Simply swap the negative thought to the exact opposite, making it positive. As an example, if it is raining and lightning outside, rather than think, "Now I won't be able to go take that walk in the park, like I planned," you can instead think, "It's a shame I won't be able to take that walk, but now this is the perfect opportunity for me to get started on that book I've been meaning to write. Today would be the perfect day to start!" Even ask yourself the question, "What is great about this situation?" or "What does this mean?" Reframe bad, or negative thoughts to the positive equivalent by reframing it to have a different meaning that **serves** you!

It is perfectly OK to feel bad now and then. You just don't want to STAY there too long, or it can affect your entire day, week, month, or even YEARS of your life! Give yourself 90 seconds to change and reframe your thoughts. Finding the good in each experience isn't simply 'positive thinking,' it will interrupt your pattern of thinking and will allow you to make more constructive decisions.

Your Challenge: Write down each emotion that you've felt in the past week, good, or bad! Then, add to your list of emotions, to create more emotional options in your life. Over the next 7 days (and even after that!), periodically ask yourself 'How am I feeling right now?,' and if it is a bad, or indifferent feeling, reframe your thoughts and experience to something more self-serving. Give yourself 90 seconds to make the change. At first, you may take longer than 90 seconds. You may even take 90 minutes! But you will notice you get better and better with time. Now go for it and watch the difference in how you feel throughout your day-to-day life!

CHAPTER 2
Physical Mastery

"It is health that is real wealth and not pieces of gold and silver."

– Mahatma Gandhi

MASTERY OF YOUR physical body comes down to two core elements: the foods that you eat and exercising your body. What you eat and how you take care of your body will drastically determine every other area of your life. As an example, if you're extremely overweight, then your emotional state will suffer. If you are obese and you have debilitating habits with your health, such as smoking cigarettes, drinking alcohol, or taking drugs, then that will impact every other area of your life as well. Health is the keystone habit to ultimate success and is the number one priority on our list because it impacts every other area of self-mastery.

I grew up being heavily overweight. I overate, I drank a ton of milk and energy drinks, and looking back it is easy to connect the dots. But when I was younger, going through elementary and middle school and half of my high school career, I always just thought that that was 'how I was.' I thought I was big boned. Whenever I went out anywhere and someone commented about my weight, my parents would just say, "Oh, he's big boned. It's just the way it is." I would hear them say that and I would believe it. It was the perfect excuse! Because of this, it took a while before I ever tried to change it.

Things changed in my junior year of high school when I looked at myself in the mirror and thought, "I need to change something. I don't have a girlfriend, I'm not happy with my life the way it is right now, and all I do is sit down and play video games and eat junk food. I'm ready and committed to make a change." I biked every single day with my friends around town, I began eating cleaner, and taking in the right amounts of the right foods. Within six months to a year, I had lost about 60 pounds, and got down to a healthy weight. The first step? Developing the belief it was possible for me to be healthy and thin.

Out of high school, I moved into a sales job

where I primarily sat behind a desk for most of the day and I began, once again, eating copious amounts of unhealthy foods and gained the weight back I had lost years before: Slowly but surely, the false beliefs crept back in. "This is just the way that I am. There's no way for me to change this... This is always going to be a never-ending battle for me... I'm not destined to be in shape..." There's a day where all of this changed for me. A mentor came into my life, who was very health conscious. He introduced me to his workout routine, and a healthy way of life. I began working out with them 3 days a week, while also adopting a new habit of 'Intermittent Fasting.' I won't discuss ALL of the benefits of 'IF,' considering you can search them on your own, and find a TON of interesting research. I will simply tell you the premise and the result. This, along with exercise, was the technique that tipped the scale for my physical health and made everything possible.

Intermittent Fasting, in simple terms, means adhering to a specific 'eating window,' generally 8 hours, where all food is eaten during that time. Simple, right? Here are some details for those itching to know what this is: Whenever we eat, the body releases insulin to help cells convert sugars (in particular, glucose) from food into energy. If the glucose isn't used immediately, insulin helps makes sure the excess is stored in fat cells. When we go without food for extended periods of time (around 16 hours), insulin is not released. The body then turns to breaking down fat cells for energy, leading to weight loss.

Over a century of Intermittent Fasting research has shown that 'IF' can lead to weight loss, stabilized blood sugar, reduced inflammation, improvements in memory and stress resistance, slowed aging, longer lifespan, and blood-sugar stabilization; ALL extremely promising health benefits, for a simple change in lifestyle. So, how does all of this work, anyhow? And how can you begin?

The general idea of Intermittent Fasting is that it gives your body adequate time to digest your food. If you eat breakfast, lunch, and dinner, your body never has the proper time it needs to digest. As a result, it is always digesting. What is the #1 drain of energy on your body? Digestion! By giving your body time to digest and absorb the food you're eating during the fasting period (usually 16 hours), you have more energy, along with the many benefits I mentioned above.

I recommend beginning with an 8-hour eating window; any time between 1 PM, and 9 PM. You can adjust to whatever 8-hour period of time during your day is convenient for you. This is typically a question for those who work overnights, or other odd hours of the day. Obviously, this may not be possible for you every day, but you'll want to make it work whenever possible. Even if you follow this 75% of the time, you will see considerable benefits. You'll eat your first meal at around 1 PM, and since you didn't eat breakfast and are only enjoying 2 meals each day, it can be a BIG meal! Then, you'll enjoy your second meal towards the end of your 8-hour eating window for dinner. Eating clean, healthy foods is still important, of course. And you can snack in the middle of your 2 meals during the day to maintain your energy. You will find that during the first few weeks of practicing Intermittent Fasting, you'll become hungry in the morning, typically during the time you would normally eat your breakfast, and around noontime. You will find this feeling dissipates, and is replaced with a feeling of great, clean energy. You will love the way it makes you feel!

To curb your appetite during the 16-hour fasting period, I recommend drinking coffee. Understand... it MUST be black coffee! Cream or sugar will break your fast, as will any food over 80-100 calories (with fruit as the one exception, which we will cover a bit later). Don't enjoy black coffee? Try it. You'll grow to the taste and enjoy it. Although, if that still isn't a good answer, I recommend sparling water! It will make you feel full and is also enjoyable to drink!

Already a fan of Intermittent Fasting, or looking for the next level of health? For those looking to maximize their grasp on their physical body, and take it to the next level, let me introduce you to Natural Hygiene. You're probably asking yourself, "What the heck is Natural Hygiene?" Natural Hygiene advocates a philosophy of 'healthy living' that was developed in the 19th century. Natural Hygiene is essentially nourishing your body with the nutrients and foods it naturally requires. This means catering to the natural digestion cycles of your body. It doesn't mean eliminating all of the foods you eat but teaches the importance of eating the right foods at the right time and respecting your body's natural eating cycles. It involves utilizing the power that fruit can have in your life and taking care of your body physically with regular exercise. Sound like a lot? It isn't once you learn the principles and live them. And it can have a profound positive impact on your life, and the way you feel.

"The human body is the best picture of the human soul."

— Tony Robbins

Before we can make a change and take action in any area of our life, we must start with our mind. We must begin with our false beliefs behind what we are trying to accomplish. The first belief to acquire is that diets do not work. You might go on a diet like Atkins or maybe even a ketogenic diet, one of the fad diets that's all the rage right now. There are exceptions to the rule; people who have successfully turned these diets into a lifestyle. In this book, I am speaking of the 99% who diet, lose weight, and within a short while gain it all back. I'm sure many can relate to this; I know I can! The real change comes when you make conscious eating and regular exercise a lifestyle.

Natural Hygiene is a way you live your life. There are some beliefs we must acquire that will help guide our decisions. A belief that may empower you is that food is a gift and must nourish our body. What impact can this belief have on our life? It will surely impact what we reach for at the buffet! Remember, we talked about this while we dove into emotional mastery. Your thoughts lead to the meaning you assign to something. That meaning leads to an action, and that action leads to a result.

If you believe that food is a gift to nourish your body, you will make **very** different choices in restaurants, while grocery shopping, and at home when it's time for lunch or dinner. Much different decisions than if you had beliefs that were disempowering.

Natural Hygiene is broken down into six key principles. The first of these principles is we must respect our bodies' natural eating cycles. Our body throughout the day has three cycles it alternates between, that naturally fall between specific times (depending on your body's natural 'clock').

The first of three eating cycles is known as **Appropriation** and occurs from noon to 8 PM. Appropriation is when we're taking in and eating food. This is our eight-hour eating window, meaning 16 hours of our day, including the time we sleep, we're not eating any foods. The second cycle is the absorption or **Assimilation** phase, and this occurs between 8 PM and 4 AM. This is when your body is absorbing the nutrients from the food you've eaten throughout the day and is using it to nourish and replenish your body. The third, and final phase is the **Elimination** cycle, and occurs from 4 AM to noon.

The elimination cycle is quite possibly the most important one of the three because during this cycle, several key processes are taking place. During this time, including the time that you're sleeping, your body is eliminating the toxins from your body you accumulated from the foods you ate during the day. Once your body absorbs what it requires, it eliminates and expels the toxins and wastes that your body doesn't need. Your body eliminates these toxins and wastes through your sweat, your breath, when you use the bathroom, etc., and it continues eliminating them until noon, when your body then switches back to the appropriation phase.

You're probably wondering, "If my body is eliminating food until noon, what happens when I eat breakfast?" This is the common misconception. So many people believe that breakfast is the most important meal of the entire day. But let's look at what happens when you eat breakfast. Many people wake up and immediately eat a big breakfast or even just some oatmeal to start their day because that's where they believe all of their energy comes from. In reality, by eating that breakfast while your elimination phase is in play, you immediately stop that phase and you rush your body into entering the appropriation phase. You've shorted your body two, three, or even four hours of elimination and because of this, your body stores those wastes and toxins, which turn into fat stores. This is how you gain weight rapidly. Our body needs ample time to eliminate these toxins!

Understanding these three natural phases our body cycles between can be a game changer for your fitness and health! If we respect our body's natural cycles, then we can take control of our physical life and take advantage of the abundance of energy we now possess. Digestion is the number one source of energy in your body. Over everything else, digestion requires the most energy. Natural Hygiene is a way for you to have energy throughout the entire day without getting to noon and being tired, without getting to 5 PM and lounging on the couch because you're so tired from the day's events. You're not tired because of the day's events, you're tired because of how you ate during the day, which then takes a toll on your emotional well-being. If you apply nothing from this book, but this one principle, your life will be forever improved.

The second key principle of Natural Hygiene is eating a lot high water content foods. High water content foods consist mainly of vegetables and fruits. Eat as many vegetables as you want throughout your day; they can only help you in your pursuit of an energetic life. With fruits, there are certain rules in play to reap the most benefit for your body. Eating fruits the correct way can have a massive positive impact on your life, but we'll talk about that a bit later. Vegetables are the one thing where you can truly enjoy as much as you want. Whenever possible, choose raw vegetables, as they have maintained most, if not all of their nutrients. Cooked vegetables are still great!

The third key principle in Natural Hygiene is ***proper food combining.*** This is the second main principle for living a life full of energy. The main rule when it comes to properly combining our food is never mix starches with your proteins. What exactly does that mean? Well, let's look at most of the popular meals served in restaurants or at home. When you go to a steak house, what are the sides that most people order? They order the steak, and then add on an order of mashed potatoes and sometimes will even add a second side of French fries (I know this, because this was me!!) Now, what are those two things? Well, the steak is a protein and the potato, because it's cooked, is a starch. You are mixing starches and proteins and you are breaking the second key principle of Natural Hygiene.

Now, let's look at some other popular meals. Chicken and rice: a protein and a starch. How about cereal? A protein and a starch. One of my favorite meals used to be a big burrito bowl at Moe's. What does that consist of? That consists of chicken... cheese... rice (a LOT of rice!) ... grilled vegetables, guacamole... essentially everything under the sun that is condensed and pushed into this small little bowl, which is a complete breaking of the rules of proper food combination. Now, you might be asking yourself, "So, what's the big deal? Why can't I combine a starch with a protein?" Well, let's look at how digestion takes place in the body.

When you eat a protein, it slowly moves to your

stomach and when it's there, your body releases acid to break down that protein. After about four hours, you've passed that protein through your stomach, and now the energy you were using for digestion has now moved back to other areas of your body where it's more important for you (your muscles, brain, etc.). When you eat a starch, the starch passes through your body, and when it gets to your stomach, your body releases an **alkaline acid** to break down the starch. About three hours later, the starch is no longer in your stomach, allowing your energy to then be used for other tasks.

Okay, so what happens if you combine a protein and a starch? Why shouldn't wc eat both at the same time? If you eat your steak and potatoes, it will travel through your tract, get to your stomach and now your body is releasing an acid to break down the protein, **and** it's releasing an alkaline acid to break down the starch. When these two acids are combined, they neutralize each other, and because of this, nothing gets broken down in your stomach. This is why people have stomach pains. This is why so many people have to get some Pepto-Bismol after a big meal to calm their stomach. It's not because of what they ate, it's because of **how they combined their foods.**

While that food is just sitting in our stomach, it is rotting and putrefying inside of our body, and all of our energy is being used to aid in digestion to get this food out of there so that energy can be used in other places. For a good eight hours or more, all of your energy is now focused on the digestion of that rotting food. Am I painting a good picture?

Vegetables are the one thing you can eat at any time because vegetables can be broken down in an alkaline environment *or* a normal acid environment. It can be broken down with anything. Now, I'm not asking you to reinvent your life and to completely change your eating habits, but I think what you'll find is once you follow these principles and make conscious decisions with food, you will never want to go back. This is what will happen, and how it began for me:

At noon, you'll have your first meal. That meal will be a well-combined meal. You might have some chicken and vegetables or maybe a salad with some steak or you might have some pasta with sauce and vegetables. You could also enjoy some pasta with sauce and bread; you can eat those two things together because they're both starches. There's no protein in that equation. You're going to have a great meal and you're going to feel great after you eat that meal. You'll then wait at least 3 hours for that food to leave your stomach. Now it's later in the day, and you want to have a big dinner, so you have a nice big piece of steak or some chicken and you have some vegetables with it. You also have a salad and you put some dressing on the salad. You can still enjoy incredible meals while properly combining your foods; Natural Hygiene is gaining in popularity, and you will find many cookbooks online that cater to this lifestyle.

I'm not asking you to completely give up how you eat right now. If you simply applied one or two of these principles; whether it be waiting until noon for your first meal, or enjoying at least one properly combined meal, you would see positive results within a few weeks. You don't need to immediately change the way you've been eating your entire life. This is something you can wean yourself into. You could do two or three days a week where you eat well-combined meals, which will cause you to feel better and give you more energy. What will happen, I think you will find, is you'll begin eating combined meals whenever possible, because of the way it makes you feel. You'll begin living this lifestyle and you won't want to eat a starch with a protein because you won't want to sacrifice that energy.

Maybe you'll simply eat a well-combined lunch and you'll save your big meal with your family until dinner. It's not always possible to adhere to these eating principles. But in today's world, with the number of options we have in grocery stores and restaurants catering to all types of eating habits, you'll find this is possible usually. There's always something they can substitute out for you in order for you to follow this lifestyle. Proper food combining saves you energy and allows you to use that energy to feel great throughout the entire day, and in the process, you'll begin to naturally lose weight. You'll lose a lot of weight. You'll get down to your perfect weight. You'll have clearer skin. Your hair will be more vibrant. Your nails will be stronger and more vibrant as well. This changes every aspect of our life because this is how we as human beings were meant to eat.

What I would recommend is to stick with starches and as many vegetables as you can throughout the day and save meat and protein for your dinner. Now, I am personally not a vegan or vegetarian. I'm not suggesting that you give up meats. I enjoy a nice steak, but I also respect those people who have eliminated meat from their lifestyle. I save meat and proteins for the end of my day because it is a lot more difficult for your body to break down proteins and dairy products. Because of this, it is going to consume much more energy from you in the middle of your day if you eat proteins for lunch.

What works well for me and other people who follow these principles is eating a lunch full of vegetables, salad, pasta, bread, maybe even some avocado toast, and save the big meal with the meats for the end of your day where you won't need the energy after your meal. In the middle of our day is when we need the most energy that our body offers to achieve extraordinary results.

Principle number four of Natural Hygiene is the proper consumption of fruits. I want you to think of fruit as a magical food, for many reasons: fruits are high in water content, and also have all of the nutrients and sustenance that our body needs. The beautiful thing about fruit is we can eat it during our elimination cycle. Now, you might be saying, "But I thought you told us that we can't eat during the elimination cycle because it stops our body from releasing the toxins and the waste from our body," and you are correct, and I'm glad you are following along!

The difference with fruit, however, is it doesn't stop or interrupt the elimination cycle because fruit digests differently than normal foods. Normal foods go from your mouth to your stomach and begin digesting there. Fruits pass directly through your stomach. Imagine it passing straight through, like a tunnel), and are digested and absorbed in your intestines. Because fruit doesn't get digested the same way that normal food does, it digests and gets absorbed much faster than normal food would. To give you an example, mango or melon only takes about 15 minutes to digest, while a longer digesting fruit would be a banana, which takes about 45 minutes. Since fruit doesn't digest in your stomach, it never interrupts your elimination cycle!

I recommend eating fruits from the time you wake up until noon because they'll help to provide the energy you need at the beginning of the day, especially once you eliminate breakfast from your routine. How much fruit can you eat, you ask? As much as you need, you'll know when you've had enough. Some mornings, it's just juice. Other days, I'll have my juice, grapes, a peach, and a banana. It all depends on the day and how you feel. This will give your body and mind a natural kick-start to accomplish whatever it is you are doing throughout the day. You can eat fruits like normal, or you can throw them in a blender along with some veggies for a healthy smoothie. There are so many ways for you to make this work in your life.

Some people hear this principle about fruit and how important it is for your body, and they revert back to an old belief, which is to 'be careful about eating too many fruits because all of the natural sugar is bad for your body!' They are half correct when saying this. The only time fruit is not good for your body is when you eat it along with other foods, and there's a great reason for this:

You never want to mix fruits with any other kind of food, whether it be proteins, starches, beans, nuts, seeds, or anything else you can think of. Fruit must be eaten by itself because of what I mentioned earlier; fruit passes right through your stomach and gets absorbed in your intestines. If you eat fruit with other foods, because the food is sitting in your stomach digesting, when you eat the fruit, it lands on top of that food. It's now unable to get to your intestines to be absorbed.

Because of this, the fruit turns to acid, and it's absorbed as fat by your body. This is why eating fruit with foods can be destructive to your body because the fruit isn't serving its intended use, and you are no longer reaping its benefits. Think of all the times you've seen fruit served with other food; fruit with parfaits and fruits on your desserts are the most common I see. If you're between your lunch and your dinner and have given the food you've eaten the time it needs to leave your stomach (3 hours for starches, four for proteins), then you can enjoy fruit to hold you over until your dinner. I recommend waiting 45 minutes after enjoying fruit to eat other foods, to give it time to pass through your stomach.

If you don't give it the three hours it requires or four hours for proteins, then that fruit will pile on top of that food in your stomach and will immediately turn to acid. Fruits can be such a beautiful thing for your body. Just think about one of the strongest animals on earth, the silverback gorilla. The gorilla doesn't eat meat.

The gorilla only eats fruits and vegetables, and it's one of the strongest animals alive.

Jesse Itzler, entrepreneur, author, and former rapper, calls this principle 'fruit till noon.' I'll eat fruits from when I wake up all the way till noon. Every single morning when I wake up, I squeeze some freshly squeezed orange juice and slowly drink it. Never drink pasteurized fruit juice because the heat that the juice endures through pasteurization will turn that juice immediately into acid.

When you're drinking orange juice from the store, you're essentially drinking acid. When you're drinking apple juice, you're drinking acid. If you're going to drink juice, be sure that you are squeezing it freshly yourself. When you're drinking it, allow the juice to sit in your mouth, and let it mix with your saliva before swallowing.

Always drink juice slower. But because it is juice, it will actually digest much quicker than if you actually ate the fruit's physical form. If you practiced nothing in this Natural Hygiene program, except for the practice of fruit until noon, along with respecting your body's natural eating cycles, you will see a dramatic difference in your life with the way you feel and the abundance of energy you have within a week or two.

Now, it's important to know that when we're switching over to the Natural Hygiene lifestyle, your body is going to go through a 'detox period.'

Most of us have been eating the same way for our entire life. We have all of these toxins and wastes built up inside of our bodies, that when we make this change over to Natural Hygiene and give our body the nourishment it requires, we will feel different.

Over time, we will feel great, but your body will not know how to handle these changes at first, and it will want to remove all the wastes that it's built up over the course of time. Understand that it may be tough at first. You might get a slight headache throughout the day because of your body releasing these toxins. If it advances into a strong headache, be sure to consult with your doctor.

Understand this is a very rare occurrence. This will probably not happen to you, but I just want to make it known because it **could.** Don't stop. Continue following this process. Continue adhering to your body's cycles. Continue properly combining your food. Continue eating fruit until noon. After a week or two, you'll feel better than ever and **full** of energy.

We've talked about your body's natural eating cycles. We talked about eating mostly high water-content foods, properly combining our food to aid in digestion, and the magical properties and effects of fruit. As a result, we're full of energy throughout the day. The one thing I must be sure to mention is the importance of exercise in this lifestyle. We must strengthen our body physically through exercise. Eating consciously is amazing because that is how we properly fuel up, but we still must move our body.

We still must go outside and go for a walk or a jog or sweat somehow throughout our day. I'm not even saying you need to completely go from not working out at all to working out every single day. I'm saying respect yourself and respect your body enough to go to the gym or get some physical exercise at least three times a week, because for someone who does nothing right now, this will be a drastic enough difference to make you see massive changes immediately, which will drive you to want to continue this practice, as you notice how it transforms your life.

Some people might say, "I have no time to work out. I have no time to follow this lifestyle." We all have the same 24 hours. You, me, Bill Gates, Mark Zuckerberg... ALL these busy titans of industry have the same 24 hours. If you don't feel you have the time right now because you might work 12-hour shifts, or have young children, or you work overnights, understand that you can make the time; if you're committed. Remember the first step to changing anything: developing an empowering belief.

It's time to adopt the belief that we **can** do this. That we **do** have the time. It's time to develop the belief that we are worth it, that we are worth the time and the energy that we put into our self and put into our body because that is how we create results in every single area of our life. It all starts with our bodies, minds, and well-being.

If you don't think you have the time right now, my recommendation is wake up an hour earlier. Stay up at night an hour later. Do what you need to do to have 45 minutes to an hour for yourself at least three days a week to give your body the proper attention it needs for you to live a long, energy-rich life. For those who want to delve deeper into the principles of Natural Hygiene, pick up the book *Fit for Life,* written by the late Harvey Diamond and his wife, Marilyn Diamond. It explains these principles expertly and is where I was originally introduced to this style of living.

> *"Treat your body like the sacred temple that is; Love it and cherish it, because it's the only one you've got!"*
>
> *— Brandon Eastman*

Your 7-Day Challenge to Physical Mastery!

I want you to see these principles at work in your own life, so you may witness the difference in how they will make you feel. But, let's start with baby steps! In these next 7 days, your Challenge is to eliminate your breakfast (if you normally ate breakfast) and replace it with fruit until noon. The beautiful thing is this alone will make a big difference in the way you feel, and your energy levels throughout the day! Don't even worry about proper food combining at this point, simply focus on the first step: ***Fruit 'till noon!***

Head to the grocery store, pick up your favorite fruit choices (mine are berries, bananas, and seasonal fruits such as passionfruit, cherries, and peaches). Space out the time you eat your fruit, that way it will keep you content until you eat your first meal after noon. I recommend eating the heavier fruits, like bananas, after the others, as they take longer to digest. Eat the watery fruits like berries and melon first, if possible! Or, start your day with a glass of freshly squeezed orange juice! I've found juicing 4 oranges right in the morning allows me to wake up fully and gives me a fun start to my day. It's also a great opportunity to listen to a good audiobook, in the process!

After 7 days, when you have started your days off with ONLY fruit, take the next step and introduce combined meals into your lifestyle! I am ecstatic for you to feel the positive impact these principles and habits will create in your life.

Your Challenge: Eat only fruit 'till noon for the next 7 Days!

CHAPTER 3
Financial Mastery

> *"Work hard at your job and you can make a living. Work hard on yourself and you can make a fortune."*
>
> **– Jim Rohn**

HOW COULD WE talk about obtaining extraordinary results in life, and NOT talk about money? Money is an area of life most people become uncomfortable talking about. Why is that? Because they're broke! Think back to your childhood; in high school, or even college, how often was money and finances the topic of discussion? My guess is… never! In school, I was taught how to write a check once and how to deduct it from my checkbook: that's it. I believe that our teachers and parents did the best they could with the resources they had, and I doubt they were ever taught about money either! Because of our lack of financial education, it's up to us to educate **ourselves** on money to create a compelling financial future for ourselves and our family. Money isn't everything, but it can sure seem that way when you don't have a lot of it! If you've never hit rock bottom before, let me assure you: money is the one thing that's on your mind!

So, what can we do to set ourselves up for success financially? What does financial success look like to you? For some, it's simply having a roof over their head, and food on the table. For others, it's a beachfront mansion, luxurious world travel, and a yacht. Financial Freedom is different for everyone, and there is no right or wrong way! To me, Financial Freedom is maintaining your desired lifestyle without needing to work. It is working because you **want** to, not because you **need** to! In this section on financial mastery, we're not only going to talk about how to have a comfortable retirement and nest egg, but also how to live the quality of life you desire and deserve today. Live on your terms, while locking in your future quality of life as well! Setting up an income for life without ever working again: true Financial Freedom! Before that, however, we will touch on how to eliminate any debts we have, which will allow us to then focus solely on creating wealth.

Before we can focus on eliminating debt and accumulating wealth in our **freedom fund**... what must happen first? That's right, our belief systems around money! Just as we must create empowering beliefs in the other areas of our life, we must do the same with our finances. We must adopt what I like to call, the **money mindset.**

When I was in high school, my one goal was to graduate, become a lawyer, and make $60K a year. I believed that if I made that kind of money, life would be good! I would be able to do the things I wanted to do while having a respectable career. Once I graduated, I took online classes for political science and applied for a job at Walmart selling electronics and cell phones. This went well for me, until I realized that it was hard living on $9.90/hr. I wanted more. I applied for a sales job at a company named Cellular Sales, a premium retailer for Verizon Wireless, and continued my career there. This was a massive turning point in my life. I became a top performer, ending at #3 in sales in New York State, earning the exact $60K that I had wanted in my first year, which was my goal out of high school! I thought to myself, why am I subjecting myself to hundreds of thousands of dollars in college debt, to earn the same I am earning now in this sales job? And with a LOT less stress! It was a no brainer: I decided to focus solely on my sales career, and my results soared. In my second year, I earned $90,000. In my 3rd year, I passed the 6-figure mark. Selling cell phones! As I'm sure you can imagine, I was ecstatic; a now 20-year old kid making over $100K each year! Life is good, right? Not quite. I hadn't yet learned the lesson of 'it's not about how much you earn, it's about how much you keep!' Excited with my rapid success, and sure that I could keep up this high level of sales, I began buying everything that I ever wanted: new guitars (Gibson, at that!), a BMW, a car for my girlfriend (now, my wife), brand new gaming computers, overseas trips, etc. Do you see where I'm going with this? By the time my 4th year rolled around, I was over $25,000 in debt, not including my car. My credit cards we maxed out. I had been under the illusion I was loaded, when in reality, I was way over my head.

I remember the day I came home, and my wife Bri was sitting on the couch, just staring at me. Before she even said 'hi,' she asked me "Brandon, how much do you have on your TD Bank credit card right now?" You know that feeling when your heart drops and the blood rushes from your face? Yep, that was me. She found out. And the crazy thing was… I didn't even know how much I racked up on that card. I looked at her and said, "I don't know, like $3000?" She looked at me and said "No, over $10,000." She then asked me how much I had on my other credit cards:

easy answer, ALL maxed out! I was in deep, and at the time, I had no idea how I'd come back from this. When you're deep in the hole financially, it can look and feel like you're stuck indefinitely. Even if your financial situation is rougher than mine was at this time, please understand that you CAN make a comeback: it comes down to how committed you are to make a change. How bad do you want it? In this situation, I didn't have a choice. I had bills to pay, and big dreams. I HAD to change. I started with Dave Ramsey's book *Total Money Makeover* and began my financial transformation.

First, I had to adopt empowering beliefs. I read the book *The Secret*, which had an entire chapter on manifesting money into your life. The concepts sounded cheesy at the time, but boy did it work! Never address yourself as 'poor.' You're **not** poor. You're simply broke. There is a BIG difference. If you want to see poor, head to a 3rd world country and walk outside the airport. You'll find it within 100 feet of the door. Adopt the belief that while things may be tough right now, they're going to get better. At this point, assess where you are now, and where you want to be. What are the things you want to do in this life that being broke just won't allow for? Where do you want to go? What do you want to experience? What kind of home do you want to live in? Constantly think of all of the things you want, not the things you don't want. You get what you think about most of the time. Thinking of debt and the lack of money will bring more debt into your life. It's called the Law of Attraction. We talked about this during emotional mastery; you are a magnet and will attract whatever thoughts and energy you send out to the world. Once you adopt beliefs that serve you, it's time to break the chains that hold us back. It's time to eliminate our debts!

Your first step is to create your emergency fund of $1000. Whatever you must do to accumulate this money, it is imperative to your success. This is your rainy-day fund. This is where you'll turn to if your engine breaks down, or your pet gets sick, or some misfortune falls on you. This is the store of money you have to fall back on while you throw all remaining funds at eliminating your debts. Keep it in a fireproof safe under your bed, or a separate bank account. Wherever you can put it without touching it or dipping into it unless it's an ***emergency!*** I know some might already be thinking "There's no way I'll be able to put aside $1000, I can barely pay my bills and buy food!" I promise you; you can find a way. Remember, how bad do you want it? You cannot live an extraordinary life when you are held down by the burdens of debt. Go through your closet of old clothes you never wear anymore, put them on your local social media garage sale site.

Pick up a few more hours each week at work. Do some yardwork in the neighborhood. There is no shame in hard work. Sell the electronics and items around your house you no longer use. Go on the 'Free' section on Craigslist, pick up a bunch of stuff, and turn around and resell it. Am I opening up your eyes to the number of options that you have in today's world to make money fast? You'll want to complete this first step and accumulate your $1000 emergency fund in a month or less. Which leads us to Step 2:

It's time to eliminate our crippling debts, piece by piece. What is crippling debt? Debt with a high interest rate. These can be things like credit cards, financed electronics, some car loans, and anything that has over a 6% interest rate. You want to pay these off immediately, because you are paying a LOT of money each money to interest alone. This holds people back from Financial Freedom. Your home mortgage and student loans are usually below 6% interest. However, if they fall into the 6% or more bucket, consider them crippling, and plan on paying them off ASAP with this process. Whether you're $10,000 in debt, or $200,000, there is a simple process to help you with this task; it is called the Snowball Method. Have you ever built a snowman? If so, you know the process: start with a small snowball and continue to roll it until you have a much bigger one, which then becomes the base of the snowman. You then work on the middle, and then the head. After an hour or so, you have a full-sized snowman! Removing debt works the same way. Your task is to write down each crippling debt you have to your name, in a journal or on a piece of paper. Somewhere you'll be able to keep track of your progress. Then, to begin your 'snowman,' you are going to start attacking **the smallest debt first.**

As an example, my smallest crippling debt was a Chase credit card with $2,000 on it. My goal was to pay this one off first, regardless of the interest amounts of each debt. There are 2 reasons for this: the first reason is **psychological.** We, as humans, have a spiritual need for progress. When we eliminate a debt, it makes us feel great. This dopamine rush we get from paying off a debt compels us to continue and do the same with the others. I'm not one to go against our psychology; embrace it and use it to your advantage! The second reason we pay off our smallest debt first is because once it's eliminated, we can then take the amount we were placing on the first debt and add that to the amount we throw at the next! As an example, I was putting $300 on my Chase card each month to pay it off. Once it was paid off, I took the $300 I was placing towards that Chase card and added it to the minimum payment I was placing towards the **next** debt! Over time, you'll slowly but surely eliminate each debt, systematically. For some, this will take a year. For some, 5 years. Regardless of your past, and how long it will take you to eliminate these debts, it is our duty to do so. As Grant Cardone says, **success is your duty!**

Phew! You did it! Now, it is time for the next step: Place 6 months of living expenses aside into a separate account. Living expenses are your utilities, food, mortgage, car payment, cell phone bill, and other necessary bills you pay each month. Sexy? Not really. Necessary? Hell yes! This is your new emergency fund. What happens if you got laid off from your job? What about a health-related problem or scare? I don't say these things to scare you. I say them to help you realize that life happens, and we must have an emergency fund to fall back on if an unexpected situation occurs. Plus, now you have no crippling debts, and the money you were putting towards those each month can now go directly to this fund! BOOM! Once you have done this, it is time to establish our Freedom Fund, and create our compelling financial future.

Investing for Freedom

Step 1: Automate a plan for saving and investing.

When Jim Rohn was alive, he had a saying: "Pay yourself first." What happens when we have a paycheck deposited in our account? First, we pay taxes on it. The government always gets its cut. Then, most of us pay Planet Fitness. Right?? Why is that so? Because it's **automated!** Then, we pay all of our other bills and expenses. And then, just maybe, we put anything we have extra into a savings or investment account. Most of us pay ourselves last. This is not how we acquire financial mastery. Can you imagine if we automated 15% of our direct deposit to go straight into an investment vehicle? You wouldn't even notice it was missing. We owe it to ourselves to pay ourselves first. Step 1 is to have our paychecks automated to send a specific amount of our earnings (10%, 15%, or more) to a separate savings account to start, and eventually to an investment vehicle that will allow our money to grow and work for us. This is as simple as sending a short email to your human resources department letting them know your plan, and they will give you step by step directions. Most companies have an HR website that allows you to do this yourself. It sounds simple, but can you imagine manually sending a percentage of your earnings to a savings account each month? We say we'll do it, but then life happens, and we forget, or we don't have 'enough' in our check to do so. Do yourself a favor: automate your earnings so you don't have to make this decision each month. And cancel the damn Planet Fitness subscription! (If you're not going, that is!)

For those who truly believe they have no extra money to put towards their savings and investments (which we'll get to here in a bit), I recommend a concept I heard from Tony Robbins called 'Save More Tomorrow.' This says to start off by automating a simple 3% to your savings or investments. Every time you get a raise at work or you increase your income, add on 3%. After a year or two, you'll be up to around 10% or more that is being automated towards your future. Our future always seems so far away, but just know that it will be here before you know it! You will be happy you followed these principles when the time comes.

Step 2: What does your financial future look like for you? What are your dreams?

It's time to determine exactly what we want our future to look like, the experiences we want to have, the cars we want to drive, where we want to live, how we want to contribute to our community and the world, etc. Before we can choose how to invest our money to grow, we must know exactly what we want. Clarity is power! Be specific with your goals. Before we continue, let's talk about the different steps to Financial Freedom. Depending on when you start this process, Financial Freedom may not be a realistic goal. That's okay; you can still retire and live a great life by reaching the first few tiers of Freedom. Let's talk about each one:

The first stop on the road to freedom is **Financial Security**: This means your investments pay for your cost of living; your expenses, like we talked about earlier. This includes your mortgage, utilities, food, transportation, and insurance costs. If you retired, and all of your expenses were covered, how would that feel? Better than needing to work to pay them, that's a fact!

The next step is **Financial Vitality.** This is where your investments and passive income cover your living expenses, along with your small indulgences and little luxuries. This can include your monthly clothing costs, dining, and entertainment.

Then comes the middle of the road; **Financial Independence!** This means your investments cover the cost of your current lifestyle, completely! If you require $70,000/year, this means your investments are earning this by themselves. You can truly sit back and live your lifestyle without having to work! This is a realistic goal for anyone, even for those in their 50s. There is still time to live the life of your dreams and acquire financial independence.

It gets even better. Next up is Financial Freedom. This is what we've been talking about all along! Financial Freedom allows you to live your current lifestyle without having to work, while also affording some luxuries as well. This is a very attainable goal for our younger generations, and even those who are older, based on how much risk you're willing to take or money you're looking to invest. This allows you to take the vacations and travel to the places you've always wanted to see, it allows you to own the home of your dreams you might have seen in magazines years prior, it allows you to donate to the causes and contribute to the world in the way you see fit.

But we're not done; there is one final step. The final stop in the road is Absolute Financial Freedom. This means your investments have paid for your lifestyle, and even more luxuries that may be on your list. To be clear, this is for the small percentage of people who pay the price to reach this point! Those who reach Absolute Financial Freedom might open a school to educate on topics they're passionate on, bring their entire family on trips around the world, own a second home of their dreams, and enjoy all of the toys and experiences that life has to offer.

Understand, not all of these steps are a must for everyone. Your homework here is to pick 3 of the 5 options and choose which are most important for you and your family. Tony Robbins calls these his 'Three to Thrive,' and they serve as your stops along the way to Financial Freedom. As an example, my Three to Thrive are Financial Vitality, Financial Freedom, and Absolute Financial Freedom. Once you have decided where you want to end up and your stops along the way, it makes the goal and process a lot more 'real' to you. What once looked like an insurmountable goal becomes possible. How are we going to get there, you ask?

Step 3) Creating your money machine

You can never earn your way to success. Look at all the sports stars out there who earn millions of dollars, only to retire and throw it all down the drain. To truly become 'rich' and wealthy, we must invest. There are many ways we can invest our money; real estate, the stock market, companies, and businesses… the list goes on and on. We will not dive too deep into investments here, as there are 100s of books on the topic that do a magnificent job. When investing long term, I recommend low-cost index funds, which you can find in a 401K, IRA, and most investment vehicles. These are low cost, and long term can yield a very large return. The stock market is not a short-term game; I would only consider it an option for someone looking to stay in the game for the long haul and not touch their earnings.

Once you have eliminated your crippling debts and have determined what Financial Freedom looks like for you, and have chosen your Three to Thrive, I recommend visiting a financial advisor. But not just any financial advice, I suggest you see a fiduciary. A fiduciary is an advisor required by law to work in your best interest. Most brokers and money managers out there have a restricted menu of options they can offer you, that make them money. A fiduciary advisor can offer you what you wish, and what is best for you in relation to your goals. To learn more about investments or fiduciaries, I recommend Tony Robbins bestseller *Money: Master the Game*, or his shorter, more recent book *Unshakeable*. They go over this in detail and will allow you to be comfortable with whom you give your money to when investing.

Money isn't everything, but it is an area we must understand and master in order to live an extraordinary, fulfilling life.

Your 7-Day Challenge to Financial Mastery!

Understand where your money goes! For the next 7 days, your Challenge is to write down in a notebook or journal every purchase that you make. Buy a coffee in the morning? Write it down. Open up a new gym membership? Write it down! Buy a pack of gum? Yep, write that down too! This shows us exactly how we spend, how often, and where our money goes. Having an app on your phone to track this won't cut it. I challenge you to actually write it down!

This Challenge will show you just how much money you actually have and spend that could instead go towards your Emergency Fund of $1000, any debts you have, and your Freedom Fund! Remember, it's not how much money you make, it's how much of it you actually keep! This will strengthen your conscious awareness of your spending habits and allow you to make smarter choices with where your money goes. You know all that bottled water you buy? Imagine saving the $7 you normally spend on that pack of water, buy a thermos or aluminum bottle instead, and invest in an inexpensive water purifier? How much money would that alone give you at the end of the year? Plus, the plastic you won't be using and adding to the already FULL landfills, and oceans? The amount, compounded over 20-30 years, would be astronomical! It's about the small wins. Because the small wins added up over the course of years could change your life.

Your Challenge: Write down all the purchases you make, in a journal or notebook where you can review them at the end of the 7 days!

CHAPTER 4
Relationship Mastery

> *"Effective communication is the essence of any successful relationship."*
>
> *– Brandon Eastman*

STRONG RELATIONSHIPS ARE the juice of life. When you master your emotions, finances, and physical health, it makes it that much easier to have meaningful relationships. We also attract a different crowd once we have personal power in each of those key areas. We ARE the average of the 3 people we spend the most time around. What does your main peer group look like? How is their health? Their financial situation? Chances are, yours look pretty similar. Be around those who **charge** your battery, not drain it! Be around those people where, when you leave their presence, you feel you are a better person. And

YOU should be that person for others, as well! Are you in an intimate relationship? Maybe you have a husband or wife? On a scale of 1-10, how happy are you in this relationship? It is important to assess where we stand now, especially in our relationships, that way we know how we can improve them. We will be discussing ways to extract the MOST out of each relationship by working on ourselves first!

For fostering positive, lasting, and empowering relationships, it boils down to one thing; the quality of your **communication!** The quality of your communication heavily determines the quality of your life! Powerful stuff, right? Communication is the successful conveying or sharing of ideas and feelings. Our words, body language, and tonality all convey information when used in a particular manner. Without going too deep into the psychology behind communication, I want to touch on how we can use effective communication to positively transform our lives, and usually, immediately!

Let's start with the basics…

We communicate for 3 reasons:

1. To create or enhance a positive feeling

When we're feeling great, we want to say or do anything to continue that feeling! The same goes for when someone else is feeling great, usually we want to support them in feeling even better.

2. To get out of a negative feeling

What is the main reason that people gossip? Or unload their dirty laundry and problems onto someone else? It's surely not to make the other person feel better, but instead to help themselves get out of a negative experience or feeling. Have you ever had a rough day, and just needed someone to talk to? We've all been there. And depending on who we talk to, we can feel significantly better coming away from that conversation!

3. To create a new result

This comes down to a basic belief system: If I create a new result, then I'll feel good!

All communication comes down to one thing: We communicate to FEEL GOOD! Our goal is to feel better, and make the other people we're around feel better, for the outcome of producing a result, which will make us feel better in the future! Phew, that was a mouthful! However, we don't want to just go around expressing our emotion!

It is important when we're upset, for an example, to not just unload our feelings on the closest person around us. Instead, it's important to ask, "What do I really need right now to feel better?" Ask and you shall receive! When we ask a question, our brains MUST search for an answer. Elegantly ask for what you want, including the feelings you wish to experience! "How can I get my needs met in a way that supports my relationship with this person?" By asking better questions before you communicate, also known as having an **outcome**, you hold the power to change your entire life.

Now our common goal when communicating is to feel good and to make the other person feel good. You may be saying, "That's great, Brandon, but what happens if I'm stressed? Or if the other person I'm communicating with is stressed?"

It's important to note, that you can't NOT communicate. Throughout each minute of the day, we are communicating in either of two ways, nonverbally or verbally. What constitutes as nonverbal communication? Just a few examples include:

- Facial expressions
- The moving of your hands, arms, etc.
- Breathing patterns
- The way you walk
- Tonality
- Posture

You could spend days researching the role

that nonverbal cues and behavior play in our day to day life, but this book is designed to simply give you a taste at how communication effects our lives, and how to take control of its power to serve you, and others!

Now, let's look at a few things involved in verbal communication:

- Choice of words
- Volume of speaking
- Tonality
- Pace, or rhythm
- Accent, or lack of

So, how can you tell if the individual you are communicating with is stressed? Well, look at the many options above! How is their breathing? Is it shallow? Deep breaths? What about their posture, are they standing straight or are they hunched over, looking sort of defeated, or down on themselves?

When they speak, are they talking in quick bursts, or with a low tonality, when they would normally act the opposite? It is critical to pay attention to these small details, as they will help you determine how to interact and socialize with this person, and best connect with them. Now, there is a difference if someone is upset, or if they are upset with YOU! There, it's important to understand that all upsets or frustrations result from the **meaning** we associate to expectations not being met.

What does it take for you to feel happy? It may be a few specific things that trigger that emotion in you. However, it's not those same things that always trigger that same emotion in others! We all have different rules. As an example, some may have the rule that men must open the door for women and allow them to enter the building first. If you're interacting with someone with this particular rule and you don't hold the door, that person may feel upset or frustrated. This leaves you wondering what has them in a bad mood: it's simple, you both have a different set of rules! Rather than expect the most out of others, or hold them at our same standard of living, I'd recommend adopting this simple, yet effective rule for life: *Trade your expectations for appreciation!*

> *"Wise men speak because they have something to say; Fools because they have to say something."*
>
> — *Plato*

We can't expect everyone to live and act as we do. Instead, what if we simply appreciate their differences, and strive to understand them better? I once heard the saying, 'If you don't particularly like someone, seek to learn more about them.' I've found this works wonders 99% of the time. To change our life and the quality of our communication, we must change some of the belief systems that create upset in our life and adopt some that positively serve us. Let's look at some core beliefs on human behavior and communication:

4. People are not their behaviors.

If someone does something that is out of character, or even, in a sense, unethical, understand that that is **not** who that person is, on a deep level. We all make mistakes and make decisions that can be 'out of character.' It's about learning from those mistakes and becoming a better version of ourselves as a result. If someone strays from the path, make the choice not to hold that against them forever. It was only who they were at that moment. It happens to the best of us.

Separate behaviors from people. Say to yourself, "I don't agree with what they did, but I still love the person." You will notice the difference this makes in your life and the way it makes you feel as a result!

5. There is always a positive intent behind all behavior.

Yes, even behavior that LOOKS negative! We never consciously decide to wrong somebody, just to do it. There is always a reason the individual did what they did. They believed it was the best option; or else they would have made a different one at the moment. Makes logical sense, right? To understand this, when someone does something that looks 'off' or wouldn't be the decision you would make, say to yourself, "I disagree with his behavior and I wonder what his intent is, in his subconscious mind."

Assume that if your loved one or friend does anything, then there is a positive intent towards **you** as well.

6. People do the best they can with the resources they have.

This comes from the principle that there are no un-resourceful people, there are only un-re-sourceful states. If someone's behavior or actions seem different than who they normally are in character, help them to change their state! Have compassion towards them. To do this, while they are in the middle of what they're doing, break their pattern! Help them change their focus to something else, by completely confusing them, or making them laugh. Change the subject entirely, to where it's so odd that it makes them stop for a second and think. This can immediately change someone's state, which will allow them to access one more serving to them.

Understand also, that if you treat someone well, even if they treat you lousy, they WILL remember it! While it may seem difficult at the moment, remember that you always can treat someone with respect, kindness, and understanding. Even if it means ignoring an individual's negative comment towards you and waiting for their storm to pass. Or... break their pattern! Meeting a cry for help with another cry for help never works. Meet their cry for help with a loving response, and watch the tides turn right in front of you!

With our friends, I think you'd agree when I say we hold them at a higher standard than others. If they don't do exactly what you'd expect them to do, or what you think is the right thing to do, we immediately take a judgmental stance and seek to correct them. Especially if they pick a fight with us... we think, "They should know how to treat me well!" Judge people by their long-term standards, because moment to moment people can easily get off-track. The benefit of the doubt can go a long way!

7. The meaning of any communication is the *response* you get.

If you are in an interaction or conversation, and you don't get the desired outcome or meaning you were looking for, change your approach! Simply try something else. No great and successful individual achieved what they wanted at the first try. They tried over and over again. Sometimes 100s of times until they got what they were looking for. The same goes with sales and any kind of communication.

Too often, if others don't respond the way we expect them to, we get mad at them for not getting or understanding what we're communicating. It all starts with us!

8. No matter how thin you slice it, there are *always* two sides.

Seek to understand both individuals' viewpoints. Remember, we do the best we can with the resources we have direct access to. The other person is acting that way or saying what they're saying for a reason. Understand where they're coming from, connect with them, and adopt a solution and outcome-oriented mindset.

9. **In any communication, all human responses are a loving response or a cry for help!**

Most people respond to a cry for help with another cry for help. As you can imagine, or even have experienced, this leads to a long game of back and forth yelling, blaming, and complaining. What does that do for you, other than give you a headache? It certainly won't help you or them come to a solution!

All communication either **builds** or **destroys.** We are always either growing or dying; climbing or sliding. When in a volatile or tense situation, ask yourself "Is this communication going to build my relationship or destroy it?" It's important to never find yourself in this place! But how can we do that?

- You **decide** never to participate in this negative communication! Decision comes from the Latin word 'incise,' meaning 'to cut off from.' Cut off from any communication that won't help you build the relationship you want! Negative forms of communication can be gossip, complaining, blaming, etc.
- The alternative is to build a bridge, an emotional connection with the other individual, a way to 'bridge' through any problem between you and the other person.

Remember, once you decide to have a relationship with anyone long term, you never again question their **intent.** If you're ever off-track, clear the path to the 'bridge' and you can connect with them once again. Questioning someone's intent collapses the bridge. Questioning creates doubt in the relationship. This is why we see many relationships collapse; they consist of a lack of trust, doubt, and destructive questioning. It's important to decide to trust this person! Ask yourself, "What is the beauty I see in this person? What are the gifts I see in them?" Ask better questions, get a better answer!

This is how you build the bridge and create a healthy, long-term relationship with another human being. Tell them exactly what you want to be for them! They will reciprocate.

> *"The single biggest problem in communication is the illusion that it has taken place."*
>
> – *George Bernard Shaw*

Your 7-Day Challenge to Relationship Mastery!

The only reason we communicate is to FEEL GOOD, and to make the other person FEEL GOOD! Because of this, over the 7 next days (and more!), I challenge you to set an Outcome to every conversation or interaction you have with another human being. Know what you want to achieve before you talk or communicate with them. Know what you may be able to add to THEM. Our ultimate goal is for people to leave our presence feeling GREAT about the exchange. This causes people to want to be around us and will help us to add value to more people's lives.

Your Challenge: Set an Outcome before you engage in any communication; whether it's 1 on 1 or speaking to a group of individuals. Even to the extent of visualizing what the individuals face will look like once they walk away. Communicate with one goal in mind: make other people feel good! You will be amazed at the riches and satisfaction this brings into your own life.

CHAPTER 5
Spiritual Mastery

> **"In ordinary life, we hardly realize that we receive a great deal more than we give, and that it is only with gratitude that life becomes rich."**
>
> **– Dietrich Bonhoeffer**

THERE IS AN attitude I adopted years ago, that changed my life for the better and allowed for an avalanche of success to come my way. That is an attitude of *gratitude.* I believe when you're grateful for everything that you have, materials, experiences, relationships, etc., you allow for more of those amazingly good things to come to you. It is a simple formula. There is so much we could talk about in the spiritual section of this book, but I wanted to leave it to the one thing that has made the biggest difference for me, and I will show you exactly how to incorporate gratitude into your life, to help your happiness and fulfillment explode, and fast! Once you can appreciate something about anything or anyone, your experience of life will dramatically improve. Once you can be grateful for the small things in life, you will be even happier when the big successes come your way. And most important, the secret with gratitude, is this: When you're grateful, it is impossible to feel angry, or fearful, or anxious, or depressed. Try it! Simply think of something you're extremely grateful for, maybe it's a person in your life, or your family, or the riches you have, or your health… it can be anything you want it to be! When you have that thought in your mind, try to feel sad, or angry. Difficult, isn't it?

Your mind can only focus on one thing at a time, and when focusing on what it is happy about, it isn't searching for everything that ticks you off or things that make you sad or afraid. It's a neat way of thinking you have access to whenever you wish! It is especially useful in tense or difficult situations.

Gratitude as an attitude is also a muscle we must train just like we exercise our body at the gym. The more we use it, the stronger the muscle becomes and the faster access we will have to it when we need it the most. So, how can we strengthen this muscle? Let's pause for a quick exercise. Write down, in a journal or on a notepad, 10 things in your life that you're incredibly grateful for. They could be things as simple as the fact that you may have 2 arms and 2 legs. Or that you have eyes that allow you to read this book. Or you can be grateful for your ears which allow you to hear the sounds of the soothing rain or the voices of those you love. You could be grateful that your heart beats on its own without your help. 115,000 times per day to be exact. You had no part in it! That's something to be grateful for, right?

You could be grateful for the roads you have the convenience to drive on each day or the train that transports you from one place to another with rapid speed. It wasn't long ago when we traveled by horse & buggy or even by foot! Now we have machines and methods of travel that allow us to do more of what we want in life, and **faster.** You can be grateful for the sun, since if it wasn't there, we would cease to exist! Be grateful for the moon that gives us light during the nighttime and also allows our days to be longer due to its gravitational pull. The point I'm trying to make is there are SO many things for us to be grateful for and the more we practice **using** this attitude, the more powerful it will become!

Imagine starting your day out each morning by thinking of the things you can be grateful for. What if you took it to the next level and actually wrote them down and as you read them back to yourself, you really **felt** what they mean to you. Your days would never be the same. By priming yourself in the morning with thoughts of things that you're grateful for, you are opening yourself up to more incredible experiences you can write down the next day! It trains your brain to be on the lookout for things that make it happy. I challenge you, starting tomorrow morning, to wake up 30 minutes early, sit down wherever you're comfortable (anywhere except your bed!), and write down 10 things you are grateful for in your life. There is a specific way of doing this that I recommend, write down each thought like the ones below:

> *"I am so happy and grateful for my job/career, because it allows me to strengthen my ___ and ___ skills, and allows me to pay the bills, feed my family, and invest towards my Freedom Fund."*
>
> *"I am so happy and grateful for my perfect health, because it keeps me alive!"*
>
> *"I am so happy and grateful for the sun, because without it, I would cease to exist!"*

You can even write down things you're grateful for that haven't even happened yet! As an example, if your goal weight is 160 pounds, you can write,

"*I am so happy and grateful that I am at my perfect weight of 160 pounds and feel incredible!*"

We have the power to trick our brain by telling it we already have the things we want. By doing this, we are training our mind to look for and find people, solutions, and situations that will bring us closer to our goal every day. By doing this, you are activating a tiny part of your brain known as your **'Reticular Activating System'** which serves as 'the attention center of our brain' and is what allows us to focus on what is important. By telling yourself repeatedly what you want and what you're grateful for, you train your Reticular Activating System to search for more things like it, amplifying the effect, feeling, and result you're looking for!

I also challenge you to pick 10 things to write down each day! If you want to repeat something that really means a lot to you, feel free to do so! This is YOUR life. Whenever I'm feeling stuck in thinking of new things to write down, I ask myself out loud, "What am I truly grateful for?" Remember, one beautiful thing about our brain is it HAS to give us an answer to a question! Simply repeat that question repeatedly until you get an answer. Once you begin writing down your Gratitude List each morning, it will become easier and easier to think of things you're grateful for… there are SO many! This has become one of the more enlightening and enjoyable parts of my entire day. It sets the tone for the rest of your day and also gives you a sense of control from the very beginning. Your day generally continues as it started. How will YOU start yours?

> *"An extraordinary life can be summed up as living with an attitude of gratitude."*
>
> — *Brandon Eastman*

Your Spiritual 7-Day Challenge

Tomorrow morning write down 10 things you are absolutely and utterly grateful for. For those who have little time in the morning as it is, wake up 30 minutes earlier! If you're having trouble finding things to write down... look around you! Be grateful for the covers that keep you warm at night, for the partner who co-inhabits the same home and shares their life with you, be grateful for your eyes, ears, arms, legs, your heart that beats automatically, roads that allow you to travel anywhere you'd like, books you can enjoy that you didn't even have to write! The list goes on, and on, and on. Remember to pick 10 new things to be grateful for each day (It IS okay to repeat ones that are very important to you!) Watch the difference in how you feel each day after beginning this exercise. You will look at the world, and everyone in it, in a completely different light.

Your Challenge – For the next 7 days (or more!), write down 10 things each morning you are grateful for. It could be anything. Choose different things to write down each day. Repeating things here and there is okay, especially if the content is important to you.

Conclusion

TAKING THE ABOVE actions in these 5 areas of Self Mastery completely transformed my life; I went from having constant negative thoughts and a feeling of 'no control' to shifting them to thoughts that served me. I went from being extremely overweight and unhappy with the way I looked, to living in the body I wanted, along with the vitality and all-day energy that came with it. I went from being broke, living paycheck to paycheck, to building up my emergency fund, and contributing each month to my Freedom Fund for the future. I went from waking up in the morning feeling lethargic and having the attitude of 'time to get through another day,' to waking up, reflecting on everything I'm grateful for, and entering each day with a burning passion and desire to use it to bring me closer to my goals and dreams.

Was this an overnight transition? Absolutely not. I took 5 years to go from where I was to where I am now. It took years to research the different areas of life, to read the books, to find the mentors who could help me, and to implement the teachings. That's what this book is for: To cut down the time it will take you to achieve the same or greater result I did. Learn from my mistakes and experiences, that way you can accelerate the process to your own extraordinary life! I hope that these teachings and principles help you to make a measurable positive difference in your life; in one, or all of the 5 areas of Self Mastery.

One important piece to remember, no matter where you are in your life situation is to **be happy now.** So many people wait to feel happy until after they've achieved their goal. But what generally happens once they achieve it? They immediately set a new goal. Or worse yet, they fail to set a new one, and self-sabotage themselves to the same point they were at before they began. I challenge you to feel happy NOW where you're at in your life. You may be saying "Easy for you to say, Brandon, I can hardly pay the rent! I have such a long way to go to be where I want to be!" And to those who say that, I understand. I've been there, too! But what made everything easier for me, was accepting my situation for what it was and loving each day of my journey to get to where I wanted to go. The thing is, if you don't choose to be happy now, when will you give yourself that luxury? You will always move on to the next goal or next big thing and never give yourself the chance to be happy with your results. Be happy now, because if not now, then when? Use the strategies we talked about in Spiritual Mastery, Emotional Mastery, and Relationship Mastery to make this possible.

Revisit this book, or a specific section whenever you need a pick-me-up or a boost in the right direction. Please reach out to me for additional insight or simply to tell me how these principles have helped you in your life. That's what it is all about for me.

I wish you the best life possible; I wish you the Extraordinary Life you deserve. And no matter how extraordinary your life becomes, remember, you can **always** Be Better!

About the Author

BRANDON EASTMAN IS a Peak Performance Coach known for helping individuals positively transform their body, emotions, finances, and relationships. He has one mission: To serve  others in helping them take control of their mind and body, to obtain the 'edge' they're seeking!

Brandon works with business owners, individuals, and teams to help guide them towards peak performance, and results.

Continue your journey to self-mastery and take advantage of weekly updates, and video trainings at www.bebetterindustries.com

Made in the USA
Lexington, KY
21 December 2019

58700159R00063